Snake Train

Edwin Frank

Snake Train
Poems 1984–2013

Shearsman Books

First published in the United Kingdom in 2015 by
Shearsman Books
50 Westons Hill Drive
Emersons Green
BRISTOL
BS16 7DF

Shearsman Books Ltd Registered Office
30–31 St. James Place, Mangotsfield, Bristol BS16 9JB
(this address not for correspondence)

www.shearsman.com

ISBN 978-1-84861-362-1

ACKNOWLEDGMENTS

"Hell Suite" appeared in *A Public Space*; "Route 202" in *The Baffler*; "Fall" and "December" in *Epiphany* and, in German translation, in *Akzente*; "Landscape" and "Landscape" in *Fulcrum*; "End with a Comma" in *The Nation*; "Snake Train" and "In the Dark" in *The New York Review of Books*; "Summer Sequence" in *Poetry Salzburg Review*; "The Accident" as "Virgil in India" in *Threepenny Review*; the first part of "Diptych" as "Beginning" online in *Truck*; "Everything is a sign" and "Dusk" in *Western Humanities Review*; and "Opera" in *The Yale Review*.

The Further Adventures of Pinocchio was published with photographs by George Woodman by Lo Specchio d'Arte. *Stack* came out as a chapbook from Ugly Duckling Presse.

The image on page 59 is *All Is a Scholar* by George Woodman. Reproduced by permission of the artist.

Cover photograph, *Cruz del Camino Number 11*, by Byron Brauchli. Reproduced by permission of the artist.

*For my mother and in
memory of my father*

Contents

Snake Train

— after Khlebnikov

We settled in our ochre houndstooth seats
And stirred our drinks. We talked about the Good,
Damned Cowardice, praised Courage, and said we would

Have done much better to have lived when war
Was decent, when there was something to die for —
The future perfect, if not a lasting peace —

Or not to have been born. The high-speed train
Ran smooth as our reckonings. We sat upon
The observation deck beneath a green

Plexiglas bubble that dulled the glare and sheen
Of dusk into a botch of blacks and whites
As the train slid west and the last trace of light

Twisted, crumpled, and powdered like a scrap
Of burning paper. The conversation lapsed.
The train was pleasant, not too old or new,

And carpeted in red, car followed car
Like scenes in a play or shops in a bazaar,
While hardly swaying we moved as quickly as

A match flame sizzles through dry summer grass.
Evenings, we lingered in the dining car,
Dropped ashes on the tablecloth and stole

Spotty carnations, yellow silverware,
And tipped a lot. The canned gentility
Charmed us, claimed us. . . . Feeling kind and free,

I looked around. The other passengers
Had fallen asleep. They smiled maliciously
Like dolls, or lay there stony-faced,

While someone muttered something in a dream.
I looked outside — night's eddying blue-blacks,
Streaking lights, still patches of light fog —

And thought I glimpsed the shiny pulse of gills
Or giant outline of a black-gloved fist
Studded with stars, the knuckles bunched like hills —

Imagine! A winged dragon! It tore along
Beside us with the vague, furtive smirk
Of someone who enjoys a private joke

Stretched across its heart-shaped snout. A book
Lay open on its head in place of hair,
And its scales were clear as the gray windowpanes

Of city halls, so I could see the veins'
Inky designs, like baroque emblems where
The virtues and the vices strut their stuff,

And its scorpion tail hovering above.
"It must be going a good seventy,"
I thought, as it lumbered heavily

Past us on its little baby's legs.
Then baring the whites of its sharp teeth,
It spread its wings until they filled the sky

Like a wedding canopy trimmed with razor wire
And rose. The train jerked back under its bulk
Then jolted forward, sped on by the wings,

As I slammed against the seat in front of me
And hit the floor, meeting my friend's shocked
Eyes of blame and threat. The beast's jaws sheared

The plastic top, but everyone took his seat
And settled back in with a snore or sneeze
Full of experience and expertise,

While I thought, Saint George, of you, and how you stood
Undaunted by the dragon's brawn and airs
Until you saw the earth drink the black blood

Of its death wound. The thought did me no good.
The beast bore down — my heart banged in my side —
And craning my neck, I saw it chomp a bright

Young lawyer screaming in its teeth "No right!"
And lunge towards me. I nearly died.
But taking advantage of a twist in the tail,

My friend and I jumped into the night.
Under the branches of a cottonwood,
Beside a muddy creek, we pitched camp.

Antelope, jackrabbit, gopher, grass
For food. We kept alive as a spoken word
Or campfire's ash and smoldering peat

Keep, for a little while, a little heat.
But every one of that commonsensical lot
Was eaten by the dragon on the spot.

for Joseph Shea

Landscape and Memory

Moi qui fait profession des choses muettes…
— Nicolas Poussin

Landscape

On this road and throughout the countryside
You see it: two boards and a chewed-up leather
Strap with which they're loosely strung together
Knocked into the ground where someone died.

Rocks. The fire-tufted ocotillo trees'
Thin shadows lengthen, and at dusk a man
Comes to fill a battered coffee can
With calla lilies. Here the new day decrees

Another day, and memory decays
Unable to remember what it was
Quickened the heart awhile or gave it pause:
What settled it in this unlikely place?

What is the mind that it does mind, after all,
Though set apart even from itself, that words,
Deprived of their senses, lie like pots and shards
Lumped in the clay they consecrate and call

Up, as from nothing, some place, this countryside
Or any — the strict sand, the sleek mirage, pale ash
Blown off a smoldering pile of roadside trash
A stray dog roots around in, teary-eyed.

for Lety and Byron

Fall

1

Blue-eyed and brown
Hidden in shadow
Fall —
       Fallen
Gold gathers
Under the trees. What are
Their names? or those
Of the small birds flitting
Back and forth among the branches, in
And out, as quick
As flame, as sharp-tongued?

Why sparrows! Sparrows.
They were never juncos to me.

Blue-eyed
Hidden in shadow, you watch
Your birds plunder,
Your trees squander
The gold that gathers
As it falls to rise,
Kindling, into the air —

Your brown eyes also —

And the sky's single blue flame.

2

Until
Sun drops, wind gathers
Cloud, hauling it off

To the beach, vague
Liminal zone
Called *strand* caught

Between here and there,
Coming and going,
Between and between —

Old dump:
Fish-hooks, heads,
And bones, clamshells,

Shoes bogged down in the sand,
You turn
Away from, back

Towards dunes, push through
Dense undergrowth, skirt
Poison ivy, nettles,

And briars, to pick
Bittersweet for its bright
Red berries and bay

Laurel for its little
Puckered ones, like moons.
Orange sky.

No moon.
A fire ring and
A beach chair flipped on its side

In the white sand of the clearing
You enter, arms full,
And stop.

3

Dark. It's cold,
With a sense of oldness about
The narrow wood-paneled hall —
                                        Fall

Ends
            (In such
A vacation house
In the off-season, vacated,
With only a birch tree ghosting
A window's flawed glass,
And the sound of lake water, churning,
Of the boat that knocks at the dock) —

Though there is someone who stands
There still, back turned,
Head bent towards a match,
And the other one who,
Hidden in shadow, holds back

Still waiting — who was it? —
Wanting to be in the dark.

December

1

A heat wave in December. Blue
Luminous field of vision
Where the eye moves, dispossessed and possessed,

And you,
And the river, wide,
Almost in spate, and the tall

Black cedars, their broad
Pluming branches that front
The far cliffs, *contre jour*,

The whole cargo of dazzle
Turns too.

2

This
Parenthesis in
The weather: the heather
Still pungent, the bees
Still busy about
Its pinched flowers —

                    All blindly
Determined, enthralled,
As love is or
As justice —

                We meet
Stopped at the threshold
Of recognition, we meet
As always such bare
Figures of speech
Still trembling and
On guard.

3

The accident of things: not what one had
In mind. Yet the flawed
Edges caught
In the daily combustion of light
Will flare, remain
Glamorous as
The singular tokens of
One past.
                (Outposted
Yucca, on the red
Hills, its handsome
Corolla of spikes,
Its creamy blossoms
So heavily perfumed
They stank; the neither
Ash nor silk
Of the empty wasps' nest held
In hand.)
                But who

Can believe it in fact?
— That the record might be
Made good in the damages
Sustained, preserve,
In spite of ourselves,
Some intimacy of
Conception won
From loss.

4

But where a line is
A field opens, and they,
As if newly engendered
While we were looking away,
Cross over.
                    Full-grown
Already, decked
Ostentatiously out
In loud
Chains, furs,
And whatnot — who are they?
Shamans? Big chiefs?
Pop singers? Perhaps
Nouveau riche buccaneers?
But they have severed connection,
They have slipped aside now
Into elsewhere.
                    We watch,
And they, who have fallen
Silent or gone
Too far now to hear,
Move off farther, grown vague,
Though in sight still, and yet
Ever more undefined,
Ever less anyone,
As they continue across
The small field of their common

Observance. Then stop.
They pick up something
And then they put it back down.
Then they move on as before.

5

Then here, as it happens,
One is,
       Half-

Recognizing the other,
Like the unlikely brilliance
Of the winter sun in the woods,
Or the sparse grass sprouting
Up through cracks in the tar.
You put one hand on the wall

And it stays there. They stay.
Sheepsilver.
Muscovy glass. The lost names,
The abandoned uses, the common
Burden of the ground
We turn (one hand
Brushing the hair from the eyes)

Away from
         (Though what
Is it, goes on
Digging and keeps
Digging, turning the leaves up, the grass,
The dirt, to find
What? A lost shoe,
The taste of lime upon lips) —

Too much or
Too little. What's left
In any case is
Excessive:

The shelved
Volumes of earth's
Parsimonious annals,
Its shuttered promiscuous core.

Virginia

Copperhead coiled in the dust of the road
By day; at night
The bullfrogs booming
Out of the high, fringed
Victorian trees —

The heel of your sandal flattens the soft new grass.

How else could the world go on?

Summer Sequence

1

Haze, and summer's
Heat hanging
Over the plains
Like a pair of curtains pulled tight.

Great plains, great
Lakes, and the flat
Drab surface of one
Particular body of water

At the end of all that greatness
With a parking lot beside.
America, you —
Your —

Sad water, scratched earth,
Roads that run straight for miles
And then stop, space,
The ground itself, you could say,

It's all yours. You rise
In the great city up
From a manhole, tipping
The cover back like a hat:

A big truck mows you down.
While in the country, un-
Bidden as
Daisies, bachelor's buttons, or Queen

Anne's lace, we run
Wild
And are gone. But it's
All over, already,

Always was, however
Often we arrange
To meet in secret again
To confirm it. Here

The body politic is wedged
Up hard against
The beloved. They want
What they want and want

It still, although
They lie
Motionless, hands
Caught, tangled

In tangled hair, lie
Sunbaked, stupefied
At length in the sand
By the polluted lake.

No Swimmers.

2

Or
Construction Site. Keep Out.
Surely we too have had

Our visionary crew,
Phenomenal prophets,
Yegg men, and such....

Broad noon. A great building's
Poor shadow
Cast down into the dirt. And I heard

A terrible roaring
As of the wind, but not only,
As of the fire that issues from the mouth of the furnace

Like a lion's tongue lolling out
Like a scroll all scribbled
With fiery signs and designs,

Like the wave that breaks
Bearing its news of destruction,
Like the Earth, in its constant upheaval, in space,

While the sleek flanks of our buildings
Exhibit worlds.

3

So, comic
And caustic, each day,
The familiar apocalypses —

Work and home —
Continue:
Sun simmers down,

Boils up
Over the next
Line in the sand;

Traffic humps
The arched bridges; and just
Around the corner, as bright

As ever, the dear
Object solicits
My choosing.

4

But I come after, treading
Cautiously,
Respectfully among
The expected relics. Look!

— The blackened stones of a fire ring, shards,
Charred sticks, whatever
Was sketched or scrawled
Upon the walls, rubbed out,

Raked over, like the gloss of ashes I
Now once again gloss over
(Here the invaders pitched camp; here, for a night,
Refugees halted in flight —)

Before stepping out,
Strangely restored, into
The vast
Emptiness they —

Such is the evidence —
Aspired to.

Hermetic Poem

I drank,
So that the angle of my neck
Was altered, and my mouth,

Opening and closing a little,
Developed a crease alongside,
And I looked down after

In another direction,
And there was a woman there pouring
Water from one

Container to another,
But not looking, so the water
Overflowed.

Sunlight. White sand.
The little pebbles at the river's
Mouth, in the shallows,

And the shadows of
The branches swaying
Overhead, and the way

Each pebble shines
Distinctly, caught
In the net of water, light,

And shadow. *Your voice*
Was never your own. Nothing you ever thought
To say was your own. Your voice

Moved on, assumed
A new form.
Drums. Timbrels. The shaven-headed

Priests passing by
With sparrow hawks perched on their staffs.
Egypt. Judaea.

We are turned away. We turned
Away. I drank
And went on. You left

And came back. It was
A long time ago
I lay down in

The long grass by the river
To sleep, not hearing
Anything any-

More, not seeing,
Even in dreams,
The other figures

On the road or river
Approaching or moving away:
Not the one that is

Already too many,
And not the other ones;
Not the ten, which is tears

And water.

for Alison

Landscape

Chestnut honey, the percolating cries
Of mourning doves, an iris leaf unties
A soft white cheese. Sunlight. Scenery.
Hard as the heart tries
To lose itself, it still comes back to me,

Hard bread, though chestnut honey makes it sweet,
And olives fatten in the cradling heat
Of later summer, and grapes, and on the roads
There are blackberries to eat.
I walk and walk. A racing lizard decodes

The message hidden in a loose stone wall,
Escaping with it. The olives shine and pall
And shine again, fall crocuses push through
The leathery leaf-fall
Along the stream bed, while from a hedge of yew

Night comes, craving the milk of Juno's breast,
The doves' soft brooding, the hard bread that is best
With chestnut honey, the bed where the true bride
And groom lie tightly pressed,
And the heart, like a window, opens and is void.

for Betty and George

Hymns to the Chariot

— after the Hebrew Hekhalot hymns

I

So praise begins — song and joy
And exultation, issuing from each
And every one of the Holy Living Creatures
Who stand before the Lord and serve Him wholly
Day after day —

         Lord, they cry out,
This is Your throne, the only one, the sole
Abiding place of the most high, rejoice

In the rock as in the wind and water that wear
The rock to sand, as in the grain of salt
Drawn from the ocean to melt upon the tongue.
                              Rejoice,

Like the bride and bridegroom in each other's arms,
Night and day, within the bridal chamber!

II

O Holy Living
Creatures, you

Who perform the will of the Lord,
Overrulers of judgment, cancelers of decrees

And vows, who act
To make friends of enemies, to soothe in the broken

Heart the fury
Of desire,

On high
In the splendor of the glory of the palace

Like acrobats you perform
His will

Only, and yet
Sometimes you go in fear, sometimes in peace,

Sometimes you exult, and sometimes tremble —
How can it be?

"When the face of the Lord grows dark before our eyes,
We fear and tremble, but when it glows we glow

In kind. We listen."

III

Lovely, majestic, beautiful, flaming
Face of the Lord when He presides from on
His throne of glory, covered with praise,

Abiding in splendor, most beautiful, more lovely
Than the wisdom, even, in the faces of the aged
Or the bride and bridegroom holding out their arms —

But who sees it is
Destroyed
Instantly. Those

Who serve Him today
Must be dismissed tomorrow.
Their strength fails,

They lose heart,
Their sight darkens
Before His brilliance, they are

Cast aside
With all the others, the lovely,
Light-footed, beloved

Servants who crowd
About His throne and dance
Attendance on

His chariot while its rushing wheels whirl on
Sapphire, leaving
Those on the right

Upon the left, and those
Who came before
Now in the van, till all

Cry out
In a vast
Echoing hubbub, some

Calling, "That is the other";
Others, "That is the one";
While the eye that witnesses it all is happy.

IV

Your throne hovers,
And it does not move.

Your servants hover,
And they can not move

Your weight until it falls
Upon them.

V

As holy,
As powerful,
As feared,
As dreaded —

Such is the quality
Of the cloth gathered
Into the robe He wears
Inscribed within
And without with His
Unspeakable Name,

Visible to no eyes
Except to those
That seeing are consumed
By the fire springing
From it, the fire

In the image of the eyes
Of the Lord, robed,
Crowned, and seated
On the throne in the palace
Of His Name.

VI

King, God, Lord,
Wreathed in crowns,
Light in the spreading
Branches of Your princes,
Fire in the deeps —

From Your height
The angels topple,
The great of the earth
Are shaken from Your crown,
All that is sweet and lovely
Trails behind Your robe.
The trees are swayed by Your word.
The grass grows out of Your joy.
Your body diffuses like the sweetest perfume.

VII

Crowned with greatness and
Covered with crowns, you come
In celebration and
With jubilation to sing
Hymns to the Highest

Master of Flames
In the flaming chamber
Of His being,
Of His calling out
Your names,
Of His riding forth

Upon you, until
Who names you also
Is gathered in that burning,
Is banked up in the raked
Coals of that
Last splendor.

Stack

I make a stack, smack
in the middle of things, or off
a little to the side.
(The thing is, it
doesn't matter where it goes.)

I heap up bricks.
I build a house.
I pile up branches.
I light a fire.
I make a bundle. Of money? No, of sticks

gathered in
coming and going
about the fields in the bright
morning light after
the night's storm.

I go
back and forth
in the field, bending
or standing, turning
as if aimlessly, as if

at the same time off
somewhere to the side,
entranced, I
also stood,
merely the spectator of

such doings, and yet
went on
digging, pulling up
old stumps, big stones,
raking the rubble

away, the shards
of past lives, what remains
of whatever and
whoever (nothing
to speak of) to make

in the midst of all that
that's gone now a
clearing, a
fig tree growing
in the middle, its branches

laden with ripe black figs.

*

But whose house is this? Whose lands?
Who's watching as I
lift up a ladder to pick
the fruit? There are so many
white roads crossing the hills.

*

While in noon heat
a man walks along
with a pruning knife in one hand,
trims a weed here and there,
his shadow small at his feet.

Nothing will waste.
Wood that serves
for kindling in winter
in summer splints
a grafted tree.

Friend, half your life
you tracked day,
the light opening
on the open spaces,
the changing unfolding

of forms, the fine play
of distinction within
and among them until
it seemed, it must have,
unending, at least

until it came to an end.
Or rather, as in
your bitterness then you found,
went on, though you
had turned away.

The second half was darker:
one room
full of shadows with
old faces looking in
and out and only

a little window
in between. You'd been
preserved, you knew,
from the start for this
particular end, which was

not yours, in fact,
but only yours, it seemed,
to observe. Photograph.
Friend,
how did you get here?

You let me stay
in your house and I
have penned you in. Friend,
that man, walking
away now, is

not you.

*

Stack. Stack. Stack.
Sounds of building
(I make a stack — ?),
hammering, loud
sharp blows, a report

like a pistol, and other
more provisional, more
tentative motions,
(a saw's slow snore)
as of someone getting it right

over time, in his way.
Musical. A ting ting ting
echoing
in space, in
hearing, somehow

reassuringly, sing
how things
report to each other — are
one way or
another

warranted, promising,
as moonlight filters
through shutters, ladders
the floor, clouds gather,
rain passes, a drill

whines
far away, harsh, louder
at times, at others
quieter, and the man
stands back now from

his work and bends
forward to clear a space.

*

But that is clearing, not building,
not even gathering or discarding.
And empty still.
Distance is
silence — hill

after hill
draws back.
A car goes down,
goes up. The road
stays in place, and nothing

else moves, as in
a movie, but far away
a backhoe plunging
and scooping up
dirt it casts away.

I put everything in
one hole and it grows
deeper the more
I fill it, burying
everything under

something else. I make a stack.

*

A tower has risen
in place of what was there
where once I was.
Put one thing with
another: They add up.

The Further Adventures of Pinocchio

Thanks to George Woodman

Your eyes open a crack
to begin with —

1 *The Critique of Pure Reason*

Nose in a book
to begin with? What a lie!
Nose in a book of lies,
sniffing out a pack
of lies, nose in a crack,
in the door, the eye spies
in the darkness stories, like the one your good father,
who loved marching bands and kept regular hours,
       still tries
to persuade you of. He says
the son will rise tomorrow,
go to school, but you,
you know better than that, the old fool,
let the world go to hell,
I won't miss a single trick.

2

Featureless as a peeled stick,
I am entirely generic,
aren't I, though my nose
at times may stick
out. But already I forget myself —

Yes, already you forget yourself,
your humble beginnings as a log,
two staring pleading eyes
under a coverlet of bark
in your original sickness. Already you forget
who made you in his image —

instead of — I have to interrupt — your own
image more radiant than anyone
or thing, the mirror where all is lost and found.

3

Take me away, carry me off,
don't bring me back
in your coat pocket, hide me
when everyone else is looking
you don't notice, do you,
intricate, beautiful, and true
like a proof in math, with a perfection
that is equally your bruised
reality, proud flesh
I gaze at like a wall,
a convict scratching his tally,
and still you don't notice at all.

4

It isn't canvas spread
on a stretcher to make a flat
painted landscape for me to play
either the story of my
going to the dogs
or the no less familiar
tale of my reform
(so inevitable, so trite,
each foretold rise and fall) —
no, it's neither
a theatrical
backdrop and definitely not the school
blackboard, this body of truth
where I find myself at loss.

5

Did I stray? How is it, this thing is starting to be,
believe it or not, autobiography?
Dear Diary
entry, forgive me, I was having
the time of my life
before I knew it.
(This is a life?)
I made up a story
I am explaining to you
I am in Beverly Hills in fact
in a hotel looking through
a soiled tatted curtain at a back alley at midday.
I am trying to imagine it exactly as it is.
I am completely terrified.

6 *Philosophical Investigations*

Hitting the books again.
This says, Imagine a pain
which is somebody's, but just where
is it? and who's to say? and what? I swear
there's nothing to it. Only words. Is that clear?
Not that they aren't in pain.
Me too.
Unwitting, I draw the curtain
on the little theater
of never mind. A whole life
I'll never dream of. Who's there?

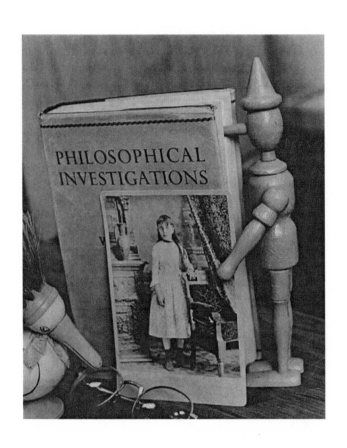

7

Mimicry, mockery,
sweet girl, dear boy,
we have a picture of things —
YOU WANT TO ESCAPE FROM THE PICTURE?
YOU THINK YOU CAN TURN YOUR BACK
ON THIS PICTURE? Oh no,
the picture's calling you back,
whether or not you want to listen or see
what's next, yourself led blindfold
      down the gangplank past
those fabled islands
of resemblance in
silence to plunge
into the sea.

Parenthesis

whose speech is a tree
in flower, whose flesh
is tier after tier
of leaves rising

upward
into her eyes, whose face
shines in shadow
like a waxing moon,

like a waning moon, whose will
is hidden
and at large, shaking
her black hair backward

in the wind, holding
in pale hands her
whole body forward
as a wave — whether

awake or
asleep, dreaming
with open eyes, with eyes
closed, always

I see her,
whose presence is
unbending, a ladder
heavy with symbols

I climb
downward, whose mouth
is made up
once and for all, whose eyes

are two sleepy apples,
whose open
heart is a heartless
chest, whose head is a nest

of vipers, who has no head,
who is a mirror shining
all over, whose headless
torso is

a vase, a voice, a flower

Yes, I am going away.

8

Catastrophe,
how did it happen to me,
a total inversion of values?
Eyes open now and watch from any corner.
And what strange company
do I now find myself in?
Bird, baby bear,
ball of string, bottle of linseed oil,
lonely doll — under what unlucky star were you born
to puzzle out this fatal hieroglyph?
Who assembled the cast of this crummy play,
mistaking a hero for the prize in a Cracker Jack box?

9

What am I supposed to do with all
these things I call
memories, but which are as unimaginable
as, say, once I was a boy,
now I am a puppet?
Blood, wine — please,
how am I to organize
all these things I wanted
and got and never wanted?
How'd this story become my story —
embarrassingly
repeating itself,
as I do ever more,
mumbler, bumbler, mirror.

10

Words are fewer now
and far between,
it is not to be expected that they will mean
what they say,
so much has gone
unrecognized away
one never had,
if that can be. Today
I met a pilgrim on the road,
who stopped to speak with me.
Pinocchio, he told me, was his name, one who had cast off love,
yet still had miles to go
before he canceled out a debt that he still owed.
He left, and I remained, in greater pain.
Like a weather vane, I thought,
from day to day
I turn,
pointing nowhere all at once.

11

Nose to nose, not quite,
nor eye to eye, and yet
almost looking at
or else
away from each other still
not quite able to tell
are you real, I am a lie,
a real walking talking lie,
but not now, now I
am listening, perhaps
I became real at your first reproach.

I —
little cry —

12

Up in the air as always, out in the open at last,
having shimmied up one strand of Rapunzel's hair
all the way, danced Petrushka's dance, that spooky tattoo
his heels beat out on the tin rooftops, run through
every story to every conclusion: you.
Luftmensch, bad boy, lollygagger —
I'm done, finished: You can kick away the ladder,
get a final gander from where
you can see it all for what it was and oh
forget it: our shadows running upon the waters
like tears, what can I say?

The Accident

This is the story of an accident.

I was eighteen. I put off going to college for a year and went instead to India, where my grandparents were living. They were medical missionaries. My grandfather was a surgeon and a Methodist. He came from East Tennessee and, apart from college and his medical training, had lived there all his life. After his five children had finished college, he decided that it was time for him "to be of service" — I think that's what he would have said. This had led him to India. My grandmother had little choice but to go along. When I went, they had been in India off and on for some ten years, years measured out not so much in days as in the drams drawn off the half gallons of scotch that they smuggled into their living quarters, defying the vigilance of their teetotaling co-religionists.

Before going to India, I had spent some time in Latin America. Poverty and misery were, I imagined, something I knew, but India surprised me. There were, as expected, the beggars, the cripples, the malnourished children with coppery hair and swollen bellies, the lepers, the cases of elephantiasis, the crowds. What I had not expected was a sense of poverty less as a physical than a metaphysical condition — not a form of lack, either, but rather part of the universal plenitude. My first night in Bombay I wandered out to see what I could see. It was moonless; the streets were poorly lit. Entering a long monumental colonial arcade, I found myself stumbling over bodies, sleeping men and women and children whose tightly packed bodies covered the sidewalk from end to end, treading upon them, I imagined for a long queasy nightmarish instant, like grapes in a vat.

At the time of my arrival, my grandfather was working at a hospital in the rather pleasant town of Kolar, not far from Banga-lore, then one of the nicer Indian cities. (I am told that thanks to the dot-com boom this city, with its airy palm-lined streets, has long since disappeared.) My grandparents picked me up at the train station in the morning and we drove back to Kolar. Mist clearing off the road revealed little silvery ponds — tanks, as the Indians call them — under overhanging trees with trunks braided from ropy roots. Big rusty orange fruit bats trailing black rubbery wings hung upside down from the branches. At the bases of trees, carved stone reliefs depicted Vishnu under a canopy of cobra heads. A man knelt by the water in a scene as classically composed as a Poussin. With one finger he vigorously cleaned his teeth and spat. A few feet away a man was squatting to shit.

My grandparents' quarters, and those of the other "medical missionaries," were on the grounds of the hospital, a leafy compound that also contained a nursing school and that was walled off from the rest of the town. The one-story buildings were wrapped prettily in jacaranda and bougainvillea. Girls — the nursing students — swathed in billowing synthetic saris with wonderful gaudy patterns, like seventies shower curtains (it was, after all, the seventies), drifted along the footpaths tittering shyly. The big iron gates of the compound opened upon the glare of the treeless streets beyond, where the passing bicycles, rickshaws, cars, and people ran on by like a piece of scratchy overexposed film.

What to do with myself? With my grandmother I went shopping in the bazaar. Mr. Ramachandra, the tailor, bounded out from among his bolts of cloth to harry her with a relentless servility, demanding that she come into his shop for tea and sweets and an interminable exchange of fulsome compliments. On my own, I picked up cheap editions of the Marxist classics from a Communist Party trailer that would magically materialize from week to week on different corners. I didn't read them. Some days there was the sound of sirens and the smell of tear gas; a temporary curfew would be imposed because of an outbreak of Muslim or Hindu rioting. In the evenings my grandparents and I ate dinner in the company of Dr. Vera and Miss Elsie. Dr. Vera was a blowsy extroverted Southern lady with billowing hair and white crepey skin that she powdered even whiter. Miss Elsie was her opposite, sallow, intense, and staring under a helmet of cropped graying hair. My grandfather sat at the head of the table. The cook brought in boiled beef and apple pie. He had been working for missionaries for twenty years and was said never to have tasted anything that he had prepared.

I thought I should try "to be of service" too and asked to be put to work in the hospital. To accustom me to the sight of blood, my grandfather had me attend one of his operations. In a hospital gown and mask, I stood by as he extracted an undelivered infant from its mother's womb. As if excavating an archaeological site, he cut through the clean layers of skin and fat and muscle, each of which was peeled and pinned back by an assistant, until he opened the womb and, severing the umbilical cord, lifted out the dead baby and set it aside. Another afternoon I sat in an anteroom preparing gauze swabs. Staff stopped at the door to peer at the sahib's grandson engaged in his unheard-of labors. A week later there was a convocation at the compound, and I was summoned unexpectedly to the stage to be decked out with garlands of jasmine for my contributions to the Lord's work. Such recognition was a martyrdom too great to endure, and my career as a missionary came to an abrupt halt.

Christmas was approaching, and in the compound "Santa Claus Is Coming to Town" competed with the distant cries of the muezzin and Bollywood hits. We left for Yadgiri, the provincial outpost where my grandparents spent most of their time. Kolar had been a kind of vacation. Yadgiri was at the other (northern) end of the state of Karnataka, a long train ride from Kolar. It was a forsaken place, a cramped warren of low houses built out of unmortared rough-hewn granite blocks, dirty, hot, and poor. In memory it appears to me in the midst of a stony waste – the heat makes it almost impossible to see – though in the diary I began to keep around that time, I describe cornfields and rice paddies and people swimming under a bridge in the Bhima River. On a stony bluff above the town were the high crenellated walls of a medieval Muslim castle. On the plain below was a dried-up tank where coolies, stripped down to loincloths, labored throughout the day making bricks. The hospital was half a mile or so out of town. The two-lane trunk road ran by and melted into the distance. Hyderabad, the nearest big city, was hours away.

Across the road from the hospital was the compound, inhabited by Yadgiri's small Christian community, converts who had hoped to escape their mostly low-caste origins. Once the hospital had been the only hospital in the area and busy. Since then, however, the government had built another hospital to which Hindus and Muslims had defected. The Christian hospital was now viewed as a hospital for Christians, which was how the Christians saw it too. It offered support for life and a place to die. A new wing had been built some years before, but the beds in it lay completely empty. There was hope that additional funds might be raised from American churches to further expand the "infrastructure," a word then new to me that I discovered was a genuine Indian mantra.

Discussion in the compound concerned health, the weather, the hope of being transferred, sightings of venomous snakes, and God. There were also the worrisome Gypsies, who occasionally rolled into the area on low rugged carts, their women resplendent in mirrored vests and heavy silver jewelry. They were said to drink toddy, and it was true, sometimes at night you could hear them singing. The fact that the hospital was rapidly going broke was not to be discussed, though each day my grandfather put on a fresh pressed white shirt and walked across the road to engage in head-scratching negotiations with the manager of the hospital and the accountant. Occasionally he performed an operation. He had begun to go blind — within only a year or two of my trip to India he would be completely blind — and coming back late from work he picked his way among the stones behind a pinpoint of light from a small pocket flashlight. A mangy wreck of a dog — my grandmother had taken to adopting sick strays and trying to nurse them back to health — coughed throughout the night in an inner courtyard. I slept under mosquito netting, which in the morning would be covered with bright red bloodstains like Armistice poppies.

My chief companion was the cook, a Goan Catholic called Das (meaning simply "servant," something I did not learn for many years). In the morning Das and I walked into town to do a little shopping, though as we walked along he explained once again that in this godforsaken town there was nothing to eat, no vegetables, nothing, only chillies. Das had been employed in the town of Bidar by an ophthalmologist friend of my grandparents and he had been dispatched to Yadgiri in the hope that he would make things easier for my grandmother, whose unhappiness was hardly a secret. For Das, Bidar was a lost paradise of plenty, and he expressed a whining resentment at his banishment from it, provoking my grandmother, a woman who expressed herself, if at all, through the nuances of an unfailing reserve, into a deeper silence of disapproval. Both of them were miserable, something for which I, a good deal less miserable but supposing myself much more, despised them both.

Das and I went to the café — in Indian parlance, a hotel — in the center of town and sipped sweet milky tea while he exchanged news and gossip with friends, though since he did not speak the local language, these halting conversations were more pro forma than informative. I seem to remember a dusty patch of a main square, and my diary mentions the offices of the many moneylenders who preyed on the local farmers. We returned to the compound in the gathering blaze of heat: By noon it would be above a hundred degrees. Along the way, we sometimes stopped to pick up something from the butcher, who worked in a pretty stone pergola with a pillowy roof that was just outside the town limits. A blackened chine of beef hung from a hook over his head while he hacked away with his cleaver in a storm of flies.

Back at the compound Das prepared lunch, grilled cheese sandwiches (the cheese came in a big can imported from a special missionary food depot in Hyderabad), which he cooked squatting in front of a Bunsen burner outside the door. My grandfather stopped in from the hospital to eat and air his frustrations before retiring for a nap. My grandmother and I sat down to read *The New Yorker*s that arrived from time to time, forwarded by my mother. In the evening, when it began to cool down slightly, I took long walks along the trunk road to admire the sun's kaleidoscopic descent through the thick cloud of dust on the horizon. My diary after a certain date contains almost nothing other than long wordy descriptions of these sunsets.

I grew more and more restless, and my grandmother suggested a visit to Das's legendary Bidar. Bidar had been the center of the medieval sultanate of the Bahmanis and was supposed to be the site of a spectacular ruined library with a façade covered in shimmering dark-blue tiles. The Sikh guru Nanak had also spent time there. I took the train and was greeted at the station by the ophthalmologist, a pale phlegmatic man who somehow reminded me of both the walrus and the carpenter in Lewis Carroll's poem. It was as if he surfaced before me, eyes bulging behind thick glasses and with seaweed-like hair pasted across his pate. He explained in his thick Virginia accent that he had arranged for me to address the local Rotary club that evening. What? I inquired anxiously. About your travels, he continued, and when we arrived at the club I was introduced to a group of middle-aged men as Edwin Frank, world traveler. I have no idea what I said, though I remember being stumped when I was asked afterwards, "Sir, what are the villages in your country like?" I didn't know what to say except that we did not really have villages, or anything that they would recognize as such. They stared at me in disbelief.

The next day, I rose and went out early, anxious to elude breakfast prayers. I wanted to take a look at the mausoleums of Muslim saints that I had heard were on the outskirts of town. They turned out to be situated in a field of soft red stone that hardened when exposed to air, making it an excellent construction material. The field had been extensively quarried, and the mausoleums now sat isolated on little tufts of ground, as if in a landscape out of Dr. Seuss. As I was strolling among the tombs, standing on tiptoe and craning my neck to see if I could make out anything in the cool darkness within, I met a young man (no doubt several years older than I was at the time) neatly dressed in suit pants and a Western collared shirt. His English was a little uncertain, but he was eager to strike up a conversation. Together we descended what I remember as an elegant stone staircase leading into a formal garden. I must have admired the flowers, because he turned to me and inquired, "Sir, in your country it is true that all the flowers are plastic?"

There was a moment — though it was not then — when I realized that I wasn't traveling in India. I was fleeing.

*

In the last few weeks before I left Yadgiri, I retreated to the hospital library. This had been named in honor of my grandmother — forged aluminum sans serif letters, brought from Tennessee, spelled out her name on the door — and lay beyond the operating rooms at the end of a long hall. It was a single room that appeared not to have been entered for some years. Inside — the room was hardly bigger than a glorified broom closet — was a steel shelf with a selection of out-of-date medical textbooks donated from a Wesleyan college somewhere in the American South. On the wall opposite, a taller steel shelf held a collection of medical specimens in cracked jars of cloudy formaldehyde: a fetus, a tapeworm, a cancerous penis. I remember a single window looking out over the whitewashed markers of a Muslim graveyard — the Bible's "whited sepulchers." It was there, at a folding table, that I prepared my descriptions of sunsets.

I decided to read the *Aeneid*, the loneliest of big poems. Aeneas is a man of the future, with his gaze forever fixed upon the past. He has been sent on a mission to found Rome, but all he is looking for is his lost Troy, its Asiatic luxuriance of sons sallying forth to do battle by day before slipping back in between the sheets to make love all through the night — a different economy from that of the world power to be, with its triumphal efficiencies. Aeneas, a founder who must lose everything — wife, child, father, lover, the sleepy steersman at the helm of his ship — in order to be given something he not only does not want but cannot even imagine. Even his adventures aren't his own; they are appointed — not so much challenges that he, like Hercules or Ulysses, will test himself against as lessons he must absorb. Dido, for example, poor Dido (doomed as she is to be made an example of): Aeneas is set up with her so that he can be separated from her and learn that that kind of thing — passion — is the kind of thing he must forsake. This is what leads people to see Virgil as dull, but it is a measure of his art, and of his epic, extending like a long, echoing institutional hall into the dusk, that the improving character of this celebrated set piece makes it all the more tragic. If Dido's fate illustrates the limits of desire, it illustrates even more starkly those of a world in which desire has no place.

The loneliest of poems — all the more so because it is at the same time a public, political poem. (Aeneas is literature's first lonely politician.) The shadowiest of poems, the least resolved, its music that of an endlessly suspended chord, as much lyric as epic, and perhaps elegy above all. As to Aeneas, he will go down — *hic labor, hoc opus est* — to the depths of Hell, where for his encouragement and reward he will be offered a vision of the beautiful Marcellus, flower of Roman manhood, already nipped in the bud. An unborn ghost. While the poem itself, endlessly polished, was never completed, and we are told that before he died Virgil scrawled "burn this" over the manuscript as on a lover's letter.

When, or how, do a writer's words take their place in the memory and imagination? What does their having done so have, in fact, to do with those words? This is the accident. As it happens, I remember nothing of my reading of the *Aeneid* in India except that, in fact, I did read it, and yet over the years poem and place have grown together in memory until they are inextricably entangled. I do remember the book as physical object, its cracked spine and soiled ivory cover, and that it was Allen Mandelbaum's translation (and, by the way, do my feelings about the *Aeneid* stem from the fact that I cannot read the poem itself, only various versions of it?), just as I remember the circumstances in which I read it, the folding chair and card table, the cancerous penis, and outside the window the trunk road evaporating into the heat under the walls of the ruined fortress (where one day, while poking around, I found myself face-to-face with a fakir, in his white tatters and long matted hair, like an apparition of Indianness). I remember the electric glare of midday and the acid pinks and yellows and oranges of the sunset, the swollen sun sliding down through the day's dust. I remember once again unlocking the Lucinda Ann Strong Long Medical Library to return to my reading.

Strange, in any case, some thirty years later, to think that I went to India and brought back the *Aeneid*.

Five Poems

Instant Torrential Rain Breaking

Instant torrential rain breaking
Out at night out of the windows of heaven
Shattering all of them and waking me alone.

I go out to
Investigate the damage.
It is not what I thought.

Beads of rain are strung
Ladders of rain are hung
Shining from every branch I climb

Rung after
Echoing rung, upwards
Through and

Among
Raftered branches pushing aside the wet leaves
Feeling the distances dissolve

At my touch entering
The night of
Maple, magnolia, fern, bamboo,

Pawlonia's steep
Pagoda of
Blue towering blossoms falling away

Soaking wet, I am wet
Through, too, chilly and shivering but climb
Still upwards towards

What mysterious estate
Where all the windows are open
Where there was never glass or reflection

What mysterious estate
Of reason and treason
Glittering *theoria* nakedly revealed

I do philosophy again.

Everything is a sign

I don't see.

       Climbing
out of the subway darkness to stand
dazzled in the long

           the ever-lengthening rays
of the sun at the end of this end-of-fall day,
a great mountain of light:

         Everything

is a sign, I suppose, and the beautiful day itself
a secret that's stayed
hidden all year
within the year as a whole, cloistral, lit up
inwardly, an amber
abstraction, filled
with shadows and sidelights, premonitions as much
as memories, waiting

as I step into the uncanny glow to take
my bearings now and discover

              everything is a sign:
the massive stone pier, the cutwork shadow
raking down sideways from the Victorian bridge,
the cobblestones underfoot,
           the dark reach of it spanning
the water, sunlight swirling gold in black water:

yes, everything is a sign, I see, and the bridge
is a great scale, balancing
on the one side lightness, on the other weight:

mass, density, utter
opacity of the old
discontinuous city

on the far side of the water, its jumbled buildings
crowding down to the docks, its streets and sidewalks
impassable, mobbed with buyers and sellers
beggars and swindlers and thieves,
while the knife grinder, tinkling his bell, makes his rounds;

the weight of
waiting; the city
you get ever more lost in, like time —

though here, on the near side, the old warehouses
are filling up with new money, new buildings shoot up
shining into the void,
autoluminescent glass and steel sprouting
flukes, flaps, fans, fins, crests, wings, fingers even
perhaps — why not? — extruded spiracles hissing
like some exotic
animal vegetable mineral
technological marvel, cocktail of ice and flame
knocking you dead or alive,
designed for growth, disclaiming identity,
shimmering with resemblance,

"like a pearl upon a white forehead,"

like nothing else, like nothing

(everything is a sign)

— well, yes, I don't see
where in the whole of this glistening, newly
rigged waterfront parody
paradiso, boasting
"more than a hundred views of the city,"
you either are or could be.

*

No place here for your three-speed
chained to a lamppost,
for your trodden-down heels and the scuffed toes of
        your boots.

No place here for your stacks of
LPs, the needle digging into the groove,
exhuming Bartók and lieder.

And no place for the profitless
"art of betrayal"
that you — that I —

all prickly
innocence espouse.
No place, for that matter,

here for me.

*

An asterisk: last
scrap of sunlight slipped
down through the girders and fallen
like a note

to the ground, last
sign of day before
night falls, a literal
footnote or

P.S. "Burn this,"
an incongruous, even
a false note, entering
the poem, except

I see *you* now, sprawled on a bench and reading —
what else? — a book in French.
Get up, your jeans ripped student-like at the knees,
your shoulders draped in a vaguely priestly shawl,

your black eyes sleepily smiling.
Night falls. The river is
black too, the sky
moonless, the reflected

lights of the city
wobble and streak
in the water like
greasepaint on

dissolving features. Go down
into that space of non-representation
forever; go down
and never come back. Night falls. It is

another night. It is another river
in another country, but the same
postindustrial — or is it prehistoric? —
landscape where

everything is a sign,
and we walk
together along the different rivers
past the Commanders' house — boarded up now —

past the power plant, turbines stilled,
smokestacks looming
smokeless; past the office park in its buzzing
shroud of fluorescent light;

past the dark barges moored
along the quay. The ropes creak.
The water laps and cries.
Night falls. The river,

voluptuary with its
litter of glitter, its unbroken burden
of broken reflections,
slips past.

I don't see.

Dusk

— after Eichendorff and Schumann

Dusk slips, wings
half outspread,
into the woods. Creakings. Clouds
overhead
dark as dark dreams. You are filled
with nameless dread.

That deer — the one you tended
so lovingly — don't let it graze
too far away.
The hunters blow
their horns. You can hear them
everywhere, hunting high and low.

Your friend — the one you trusted —
don't trust him anymore.
His words, his looks
seem true, but in the core
of his heart: nothing,
only war.

What sinks tonight
exhausted to the ground
tomorrow will rise
renewed. In the dark, though,
things are lost that are never found.
Hold still. Say nothing. Sit tight.

Dreams, stones, absence, silence

and night: for this is
you, isn't it,
indisputably, as
it is I who am lost
without you —

End with a Comma

End with a comma, the end
The more decisive because
Inadvertent, broken off,

The implied
Clause, whatever
Qualification or

Continuation had been
Intended, thus
Unappended, unsaid;

Call self-
Referentiality a
Trivial property, a mere

By-product of
Formalization, meaning nothing,
And admit it is not reflection that counts

But connection: The fact is
I could not get clear, I could not get clear
Of myself.

Dispense with images.
The mirror wants to be real.
You are missed.

Say more than I can say,

Hell Suite

— after Montale

1

You know it: I
Must lose you and
Cannot.

   Each
Gesture, each
Voice, even
The salt on the breeze that darkens the spring sky
Over the flooded wharves
Next to the waterfront arcade:
Each targets me, a dead shot.

Iron landscape. Forest of masts.
Dusk sifting like dust.
Like a fingernail raking glass,
A shriek goes up in the distance and goes on.
I search
For the sign that is
Lost, the solitary
Token of
Your presence left
To me.

   And Hell —

      Hell is the one true thing.

2

Pastimes of Hell. Blaring loudspeakers emit
Shrill bursts of static around a congealed mass
Of every stripe and color. Buses spit
Their contents out. Above the seething abyss

Heat shimmers and little curly plumes of smoke.
A spotlight broadens like a river; a crowd
Gathers to cross. A second light splits the dark:
A black guy, snoozing; loose women making loud
Advances, looking sharp. "Buffalo," I muttered —
Dumb, and yet immediately the spell took.
Where the blood deafens and the eye is lightning-forked
And nothing changes, I heard the pistol crack,

Saw milling legs and every bent striped back
Go surging down the track.

3

Rain spitting, splattering
Against the hard
Magnolia leaves;
Rolling March thunder; hail —

(Crystalline tinklings in your nocturnal nest
Catching you by surprise, and the dimming gilt
On the mahogany, on the spines of the leather-bound books
Like a grain of sugar in the shell of your eyelids still
Burning)

       Lightning, split-
Second eternity, whitening tree and wall,
Catching you by surprise; marble, manna,
Cataclysm — sentence that you carry carved
Within you and that binds you to me more
Than love, strange sister.

Brawling. Yelling. Sistrums. Tambourines
Rattling down in the ditch of thieves, the stomped
Fandango, and in the air a gesture groping
Up...
          While you —

(Clearing with a wave of your hand the cloud
Of hair out of your eyes) —

You turn into the dark.

4

Not wanting life to pass
The swallow brings the blade of grass,
Though all night long the rank
Water leaches at the stone bank.
Torches smoke. Once more
Shadows straggle up an empty shore.
The saraband wheels
Around and around the square to the
      rumble of paddle wheels.

5

It seemed such an easy thing
To make of the space
Lying open before me
Nothing, a nothingness,

And equally, the pure
Focus of your flame —
That was something to transform
Into my tedium, my stupor.

Now, though, that nothingness fills
With everything I felt
Too late: I feel the blunt
Dread in which I wait

To serve you. But only the light
Of your own eyes enters your sight.
From a balcony you lean towards it
Out of a darkness that does not blink.

Opera

Die Meistersinger *misremembered in two broken parts*

FIRST PART

Things stand out
in the light
of that measured space
distinctly.

          He has stacked
the wood beside him: It lies
at hand. He has settled
the tools on the workbench
and they are ready. He has rolled
his sleeves up neatly
to greet the morning shining
in the window of
his little workshop where

all darkness is swept aside.

*

What do we see?

Ordinary things! What else would we see
in this renewed cleansing extraordinary light
but the ordinary: things —

wood that discloses
its bright workable pith, its fine
grain free of knots
like muscle, the hand's

own muscle, the steel
edge of the adze
dully glinting in hand,
the hand itself on the handle, the handle gripped
      in the hand —

and the world outside
beckoning to us: the meadow,
the tree that stands,
wind blowing on the hill.

These are the things that we see.

*

And hear. For he sings

now. He lifts his voice and he sings
about it, in praise of it, sings it up and in
and out of thin air,
his materials, his tools,
each with its proper application and weight,

and his particular poise, that too, his achieved
self-possession, his wealth,
his world —

all this he sings and as he sings he can hear

his children singing, the distant voices
of boys and girls all calling back
and echoing his in familiar response —

*

though he looks up now and
breaks off: now
sees himself
bent over his labor growing
old in them, face withering, voice
faltering, *his* voice cracking and dying —

＊

yet hears for all that
in the children's voices carrying forward in time
his own voice calling him back to himself
across the delay of time keeping time
in the round of their days

                  he thinks now as he
turns back to his bench, absorbed once again
in his work, yes, and knows
this is
as it should be and is
eternity, in which

the fathers and mothers
the sons and the daughters
are gathered together in the here and now
and then and there and everywhere singing
the one great chorus again and again
returning to its unaltered refrain

of pure confirmation

                  of the opus, the work

that completes us, that makes us
free in the encompassing meadow to sing
a song that is not just a song but a language,
a language of song that is pure conjugation
in time of these things, the workbench, the wood,
the hand and the light and the world all arranged

in an order at last no other than life.

SECOND PART

To be sung in the key of I, oh
Yes!

It is no key, I know.
It is no key I know.

To be sung, that is,
In no key. Aieee!

＊

Lean mouth, scrannel flute,
Revisit the charming scene above
As antithetical fantasy,
Thus proving it to be
Fantasy pure and simple.
A sick one.

＊

He and His who think
To make a mockery of me
I mock in turn.

I interrupt them.
I copy — no — ape them.
(Let's call a spade a spade.)

I play back to them
Their seedy revelry
Both in my deep groaning

Natural tuneless voice
But also
Falsetto,

My voice shrilling and trilling
As after
Sucking helium out

Of a balloon, voice rising
Higher and higher,
Like a dirigible now,

Now a child's squeaky voice, now an excited woman's,
Never a real man's, impersonal now
As the sun, as the great

Law itself shining high in the sky
Above the great field where I – only I –
Have gathered them all to witness my

Escape.

*

I the intruder, the gratuitous one,
I stand out. I
Stand outside, denied.

Music I make, but the music I make
Is never more (or less)
Than the bare

Rudiments of music, a mere
Bowing and scraping.
I don't sing.

I don't perform.
I practice
Endlessly

Upon you,
Poor politician of my own renown
With all my hopeless designs.

I do scales, yes,
Creaking from step to step.
I sprout scales, bedraggled dragon.

I choke. Always I choke.
My attack decays.
My decay attacks.

My voice cracks.
My voice is a crack.
Oh tell me, It must give pleasure.

*

I say, I
Argue even (I am
Without shame of course):

Don't you need me? Don't you
If only to
Define yourself

In opposition to me? And who in fact would you be
Without me
To anathematize, to despise

If only as a piece
Of bad logic, a German professor
Of music, a stock

Comic figure, though even as such I am
A little tired, meant to provoke
Not laughs so much as groans. *Vieux jeux.*

*

I am of course The Jew.

*

And I am of course the true
Producer of this show.
There are no tools on my bench.
I bring you to mind.

I am the director and I am the actors
In the little scene I stage.
I play every part
And yet I stand apart.

Within I am without.

I am the critic.
I come before and after.
I make points.
I repeat myself.
I go on.
I stand here representing
The impossibility
Of any form
Of expression or

Communication
Whatsoever.
I am a cliché.
I am absolutely modern.

*

I am the fear
You all feel hearing
The music:
That it will go on;
That it will stop.

*

Yes, I
Stand out-
Side, and it is
By virtue of me
They emerge
In their purity, their
Unity, the happy
Common consent of
Mingled voices rising
Up and up,
While I, yes I,
Am falling, falling,
Through the endless space
Of a single note
Never to be repeated.

*

One Two Three: We
Are gone, all gone
Together
Forever. I

Sing thus and thus.

Mirror

Wait

Wait, first,
for what will happen next.

Set the scene.
Strip the branches
of their accumulated
weight of leaves, leave

for a sign only
a perfunctory
notation trailing off

on bare sky, *tree*.

*

Not that.

I clutch a stub
of pencil backward
in my fingers, scrub
the paper clean.

Next scene.

*

Not then these
successive, unfolding
days of cold rain
that go on, as I do,
too long, already too long....

*

Then again, trees —
their stripped
branches, bare
illegible decrees
scrawled — staining —
the dirty sheets of sky.

What's left?

Things
lessening, loosening,
dropping down, gathering
on the ground: they rot
and return, seeming the same,
though not.

Then today, clouded and gleamy, as if
caught in a peeling mirror: the rain
falls through it and is rain
for real, stinging my cheeks.

Shoes tread

the heaped sidewalk, shit-stink
of gingko fruit slick
on the sole. Shoes slop

through brimming gutters, one yellow
leaf-scrap at the tip
of each rain-wet shining toe.

Out of its split green spiny carapace,
the chestnut bulges, glossy,
dark as a horse's eye.

Gingko again: leaves like
little gold fans fallen
to the ground – the ground
of a medieval altarpiece.

                    What's left

to kneel down to in the growing
disaster, kneel in the wreck,

and what will last and what will be the last
thing of all, final
residuum, stubbornest stain, or faint
footfall crossing the threshold before the door's
shut, echo of fall's

unending questions of glut and dearth
returning unanswered to earth?

Diptych

I

She appears. She hurtles
Out of the heavens. Out of the blue, she falls

Hard, heavy as can be, as unforeseen
As foreknown, she

Plummets and
Plunges down, she comes

Spiraling in towards the high branches lifted
To intercept her, to catch her, to claim her, she rips

Right into them, whirl and whistle, crashing
Into the crown, smashing

Down into the
Canopy, spinning

Inward, exploding
Outward as

A welter of leaves, so many twigs and branches
Shorn away sharply, cracking, or flailing

Back into place as still
She drops on through them, then stops, then drops

Again, and with
A lurch and a jolt and the shock of coming up short now

(The tree
Shuddering and rocking but already rocking

Less, the whole
Shock of it — her

Sudden passage
Into and out of sight —

Resolved now down into the roots from which
Unmarred, even

Unmarked, the tree
Rises) she falls

To begin with. *To begin* —

II

Now she is of it,
Inseparable from
The tree, its branches,
In early December,
Just on the brink of winter,
But already bare and striped
With snow —

And she is of it,
Fallen among those
Leafless branches
To become
Part of them,
Although not as in Ovid
Identical with them,

No, present instead
As a difference that is
Indifferent, an
Ambivalence even
Within the one and the other
And within, for that matter,
The eye

That observes, the eye,
That in looking looks
Away and in
So doing sees it, seizes
That double presence —
Tree, woman,
Woman, tree —
Each, you might say,

Not so much mirroring as
Mistaking the other.

(And here it is Ovid, unlucky
Poet banished
To the end of the world
And edge of the Black Sea
Who steps into
The next stanza to observe,

As if mistaking were being?
And, *Yes*, Ovid answers,
Yes, it must be.)
But now the eye, left

To its own devices,
Prophetically
Reviews the course of the year
And years and sees them,
Tree and woman,
Woman and tree,
Disappear
Again in the flicker

Of new leaves only
To reappear
As the wind sharply
Pares the leaves back
Leaving the branches bare
Again and the image
Restored to the eye.
She is, they are,

I see, and Ovid
(Though no one hears)
Will lift his voice to cry,
The distance in which
We appear at once
A part of it
And apart from it

And disappear

And so beneath the wheeling sky
And sequent arches of the sun and moon
And storm and cloud and ice
And smoke and mirrors
Always remembering those limbs unbared
At length in the bare branches of the tree
And Ovid at the bitterest end of fall
Sentenced to walk apart
And so forth
Over the Black Sea shining blue
Between the spare lines of this archaic craft —
And so forth. (And so on.)

Route 202

Somehow we are always back
on it, though always
it appears to be going a different way —
here, east-west; there, north-south;
anyway the wrong way —

and there is nothing much to see,
mainly the scrawny late-growth woods
that famously cover up the abandoned farmsteads
and well-forgotten setbacks of
earlier passersby, our ancestors, or we halt

at the granite crown of a hill
as worn down as an old tooth
affording a glimpse of another road
(it must be the very one we want,
the one that goes to the place where we are going,

if only — if only! — we could get there, we laugh)
and the gas station nestled in the valley below.
Old potholed manufacturing towns,
weed trees, sagging row houses, Irish bars:
It is all very familiar

and everywhere much the same
here on the road through history to where
history ran out
with us alone on it, it appears, and though we are
quite lost we admit now, we are barreling along

happily enough in silence when again
that sign crops up, Route 202, the same,
my mind wandering as it does to wonder
at the two identical twos facing each other
across the empty space of the zero, just like

a mirror, I think. And oh yes, it is our road after all.

for Jill

Anti-lyric (Marsyas)

Me as you see
Me now:

    Me

Hanging lashed-up by
My ankles down
In an ostentatious display
Of dumbstruck dismay
At the God's surprise
Parting gift:

      Me

Left to cure in the heat, a scrap of meat
For the jackals to worry, a bone
Of contention
In a black
Parliament of flies, spreading
Like a disease
The dirty trace
Of that terminal disgrace,
My art:

    Me

Who under the God's
Strict tutelage mastered
The whole repertoire of
Howls and whimpers, from those of the damned to those
Of the newborn, and – Oh

Virtuoso! — never
Failed to hit the wrong note:

                    Me

Transformed
Utterly
Into Your instrument, my skin a flapping
White flag, my rent
Body Your
Imperial purple tent:

Me, facing the earth
At last for all I'm worth —

And yet here the sentence
is reversed. Night falls.
A countermovement begins.

Out of their hiding places the dispersed
company of halt
rhythms, despised

rhymes, now
reemerges, so many
nameless shadowy

creatures creeping
in straggling lines
into the clearing where

silently they
unstring from the branches
of the tree the carcass

and carry it away.
In the void where
no light comes and no

god can penetrate
and even memory fails,
unobserved,

it is buried.
Where it is buried, I
take root and grow.

My song remains —

In the Dark

Further information is sure to be
forthcoming, but for now
our one
recourse is
to wait, and we,

we have been,
we have been waiting now
for a very long time
for something
to become clear, although

everything remains
unclear. The light,
even the light is —
dim like the light in a basement — and these
shambolic trees

with their nearly identical trunks
tubular as organ pipes and above,
instead of leaves, a mass
of wispy shadow,
reminding me of a feather duster, at least

if you were lost in one —
do you recognize them? Are they pine trees or some
deciduous or
ridiculous species,
and is it dusk or dawn or an overcast day,

and has it stopped or started or never been raining,
and are we inside (looking out through the screen
of a screen porch in a cabin somewhere in the woods
on vacation) or out?
No one can say,

and yet just now it appears
we have it may be
by chance or perhaps
by secret design arrived
at a picture. Oh no.

We have stepped into the picture.
That's where we are.
The trees are painted and the leaves are painted
and the water is painted
poorly. Did

I mention the water
before? No, it
has just become clear,
or rather murky. Gray,
gray as cement, and yet

vaguely giving (tap it,
it will answer like
a drum), this is
water to walk on
not as miracle but

in fact, and we are
walking on it. Walking on water,
we have crossed over the lake,
leaving the previous stage we were at
in the background in order

to enter the background
itself. Here
things loom up,
things trail off in a haze,
and everything is more or less out of scale,

with the detail, like
an eye seen up close,
either blurry or gross,
and being here, in the background, we have
become once again

unclear: Just where
are we in that
blot of what
if you were feeling generous might
be a hillside or not?

It seems we must wait,
must still wait,
must wait even longer
for clarification, but no,
no no no no no, now I see

how it is: There is
a hole in this picture
where we are.
There we are
and might settle down,

might even set up a town
by the name of Good Luck
in the state of Contingency
in the country of
Impossible to Say —

isn't it, anyway?
Yes, nothing is clear,
and yet for all that we will go
on waiting among
the fugitive colors, faint trees, ambiguous

formations, and shadowy reaches of this
picture become abruptly as real
as we are, perhaps. We
stop. We are
astonished to be

in the dark.

Notes

HYMNS TO THE CHARIOT
The Hekhalot hymns date from third and fourth centuries C.E. My versions are based on T. Carmi's prose translation in *The Penguin Book of Hebrew Verse*. Carmi explains that the hymns "were composed by the *merkava* mystics in Palestine and later in Baylonia. The *hekhalot* ('palaces') are the seven heavenly halls through which the visionary aspired to pass; the *merkava* ('chariot') is the divine throne, situated in the inner recesses of the seventh heaven.... The mystic is instructed to recite [the hymns] in his ecstatic ascent to heaven."

THE FURTHER ADVENTURES OF PINOCCHIO
Around 2003 George Woodman began work on a series of photographs incorporating a small wooden Pinocchio figurine (painted a uniform green) of the sort found in tourist shops throughout Italy. My poems were written in response to his photographs. The poems and photographs appeared together in *The Further Adventures of Pinocchio / Pinocchio: Le ultime avventure*, which came out in English and in Italian (translation by Anna Cenni) editions in 2004.

The story of Pinocchio is well known. He begins as a log that is miraculously imbued with spirit and personality; is fashioned by the woodworker Geppetto, his devoted and long-suffering "father," into a puppet; promises to go to school but instead plays truant; succumbs to repeated temptation and lands in numerous scrapes; degenerates morally until he is turned into an ass; repents, regains his puppet form, rescues his father from the mouth of the whale (literally), and at last wakes up to find that he has become "a real boy." Pinocchio enjoys the good auspices of the Blue Fairy, his guardian angel, a figure who is at once mother, sister, and beloved and who slips freely across the borderline of life and death.

In the sequence, Pinocchio takes a particular interest in philosophy, at least to begin with. Here and there, he addresses the Blue Fairy, who on occasion also speaks.

DUSK
Eichendorff's poem is the tenth song in Schumann's *Liederkreis*, op. 39.

HELL SUITE
Though the poems derive, with greater or lesser degrees of infidelity, from poems by Montale, the sequence is my own.

OPERA
In 1993, I attended a performance of *Die Meistersinger von Nürnberg* at the Metropolitan Opera. It was the first time I had seen – or heard – the opera, which revolves around a singing contest and is both a musical drama and musical manifesto about the nature of music and its relation to society, history, and, *über alles*, Germany. I was struck by the extraordinary interplay in the opera between the "true" music of the venerable Hans Sachs and of the young genius Walther and the "bad" music of the pedantic Beckmesser (taken by some critics to be an anti-Semitic caricature) and how it subverted the very distinction that Wagner seemed to intend. I worked on the poem for a number of years, in the course of which I accidentally, and for the purposes of the poem, irreversibly, transformed the cobbler Sachs (a historical figure) into a woodworker.

Thanks

to William Alfred, Byron Brauchli, Katie Browning, Elizabeth and Robert Chandler, Jaspal Chatha, W.S. Di Piero, Monroe Engel, Barbara Epler, Robert Fitzgerald, Tony Frazer, Beth Frost, Peter Gizzi, Wolfgang Görtschacher, Jeffrey Gustavson, Richard Howard, Brigid Hughes, Immy Humes, Katya Kapovich, Michael Krüger, Agnes Krup, the Lannan Foundation, Wendy Lesser, Dr. and Mrs. Carroll Long, J. D. McClatchy, Andy McCord, Melissa Monroe, Anna Moschovakis, Philip Nikolayev, Michael Palmer, Elise Partridge, Erik Rieselbach, Joel Rotenberg, Michael Ruby, Anthony Rudolf, Jill Schoolman, Akhil Sharma, Joseph Shea, Lee Siegel, Robert Silvers, Stephanie Smith, Ben Sonnenberg, Bill Stahl, Linda Trimbath, Betty and George Woodman, Matvei Yankelevich, Gus, Emma, and – *ave atque vale* – Alison.

3

Rain, spitting, spluttering
Against the hard
Magnolia leaves;
Rolling flood, thunder, hail —

CPSIA information can be obtained
at www.ICGtesting.com
Printed in the USA
FFOW03n1129090415
12459FF